About the Author

I met this fabulous business man who still wanted to be friends with the world. I know all about his relationship with his dad which wasn't so cool but a lot interesting. And his daughter who he is fighting for, her custody like a usual phenomenon happens to this society. A hero for a lot of labours. Yet thriving alone for justice to his love story. The minute I met him I knew he his quite a steam at culture. Wherein I could only meet him for shopping and lunch, the shopping I did was for myself. I have never shopped this much. I am trying to write here about the author even though I am writing the pages it's all I learnt from him. Trying to miniscule the lecture into a literature. The genius nature in him is from his childhood. You all may get surprised but he was a brilliant student. Too brilliant for a business man that makes him too intellectual at relationships. He acquaintance you as if your life is going to get charmed up. He has a family but it's so huge that of an arm to hug. There are several kids who kind of has his devoted attention as they are special by birth. I am also one of that kind of custody since my speciality is minute I could call him my soul best friend. The fun the care the belonging is so comfortable because I kept fighting for relationships everywhere still I found a balance in him. I know that he is contented with whatever he has. He owns a beautiful car and I have taken a ride in it. I demanded the hero out of him and he turned into a superhero. The leverage of this study of a businessman is why to make you understand what the book is preaching ahead. Each word is coagulated as the jurisdiction of his analysis to certain things which are sophisticatedly comes from nature. The very upbringing is so neat that his fights with his dad is worth a knowledge. He might have made a remark on people through those fights. Eventually I will pray for his union with his lost family and also that our country should have businessman like him. That I also I pray for. I would like to introduce you to the silent author of this book. Because it's the study of him I am putting forth on the papers. I hope you enjoyed my journey of this fantastic man I met in my life so that you can carry on reading this funny book. Actually, speaking of business I have studied my degree in that and I know that he Is somebody who is quite good at it. I must challenge my livelihood for him one day where I get to be a part of it too. I am hoping that this acknowledgement will bring you literary that is directly from a mind of business man who you rarely catch up with because they are like ghosts. Envelope in your knowing of this person so that you can connect to the book I wrote.

Here, I will tell you something about myself. I am a trapped ancestor of kings & queens in a tale of rejected girls from a fairy tale. They were expelled from a clean society. Perhaps I still have a walk through the circles of love story. He somehow managed to escape me from such revelations which will tell me that I am morally an orphan. The key to my flat is going to be a gift from him too one fine day. I will have a work and call it as a job which will be solely mine from him. That my neck won't be down and be in grief or guilt but I will fly with my wings, wings of studies, art and friendship which I found in him. The belief I had on myself I happen to think that it is also my discovery within myself and he keeps it safe. He lets me trust myself and love myself. He tells me I am an Angel and I happen to fall for him. I happen to become one for him. A fallen Angel. That my life is full of enthusiasm and confidence which was healed by him. I also wrote this as a case study of my own being that I deserve to live a life made of love and stories and happiness. I am so light hearted that I can simply gell with people I meet and have a very nice and peaceful longevity. It's all because I found a gem just like a treasure in him. I forgive that's why and I know that forgiving helps in making this strange locks of homo sapiens live. They should live for a love story. The only deed which we have got to do seriously. That path is visible to me always. I want to guard it with my life. I am used to be an angry person and he beats that anger inside of me. That's how that anger is now calmed up. There might be the last of angry emotions which I got it out on him. I am sorry too. I am sorry for the things I should be for. Such kind of person when enter your life you actually feel that some one did really enter. They make it feel like and look like gifting. Gifts are those objects which you make you immensely happy. They take care of you. He takes care of me just like he is a gift and top of it, he is a business man and I willingly want to call them "Gifts". Then there were days I was completely lost of the past happenings and I just happen to tell him that, he made sure he equalled the pain and come to me like that. I could tell him the most important thing was that , I could confide with him what I couldn't even share to my family. I might be a small potion of fairy tale however broken it is but he still have the decency to protect the injured fairy inside of me. That little fairy is helping him. In every day business we speak often and every call is a dose of togetherness which I hardly got in my life span. I might have caused myself a disease of forgetfulness yet I want to remember him always. The spirit of nature is also healthy these days. I have started watering a small plant , due to the vase and it's size that plant has become bonsai. I am also like that in his life. He waters me daily. Anyway how much a person means to you is added when you fall in love. Each bondage each person will be freed from your life just to give you enough space. To fall in love. They all become your study which u involve in being in love. I met a guardian so secluded by insults and irresponsibility. He is a perfect father and a loyal husband too in his day to day life. Let's make the business man a little famous as it is he is busy always he won't be less visible here because I have captured a memory.

Written by:
Purvee Singh Bais
Author of the Book of Fairy

Dear Marriage

You are born in a promise. You grow on my devotion. Your are a success if feel fortunate reflecting myself in you. Your happiness creates recognition. Your responsibility is to make me feel free in this union. You elevated me to we. You are dead if I think too much of me in us. Your life is sustained if I nourished you more than you nourishing me. Your battle is always with emotions. I hope I am blessed with a mighty intellect to gain access to wisdom to win those battles. After every battle, I realise you win only if I lose for us. Your joy is in making me feel royal in you for me to be loyal to you, only then I shall happily drown myself in servicing you without any compromises to the promise.

Dear Name

You are born in my intellect due to memory. You grew on me by mother's calling. Your success is in recognition not in your pronunciation. Your happiness is in your achievements. I am obligated to be in devotion to you as long as you make me feel fortunate in associating with you. You are reborn in battles if you manage to win every battle. I feel lucky when you are talked about in communities. My wish is to learn about the me while being you. Your form gets dissolved eventually leaving behind your actions to create a new name for me.

Dear Money

Your purpose is to feed my needs not wants. With you next to me, I go through experiences to grow my intelligence. Along with those intelligence comes impressions which are due to my attachments with you. You success is reflected through my peace at sleep. Royalty is what you make me expect for my happiness; but it is only possible, if you are at service to me, not if I am at service to you. You are famous if you are spent responsibly, you are also famous if you are spent irresponsibly. Your expense is directly proportional to my courage. If your death brings more skills to me in learning then you never really die. Your battle is for the recognition in your community. Your wish is to make me feel free but I am only freed when I am free of you. You eventually dissolve and reveal the true nature of my soul. That's the end of your journey with me.

Dear Speech

Your were born out of communication for communication. You feed on my emotions if you are a gossip & you feed on my intuition if you are truth. Your success is in your expression of intelligence in your creation. I am at peace if you are used by me responsibly. If you truly reflect me, you appear happy. You are responsible for servicing my fear & courage. Your enemy is ignorance, you need transcendence to sharpen your intelligence. Your truth is often challenged for its ambitions. If you survive, you will be fortunate to command a larger audience bringing you recognition. You will win silence only if you wish to express my truth. In the end, you are drowned in your gossips or you come again to communicate the truth.

Dear Wish

You are born from my ambitions. You feed on my silence by wanting more. Your success is only possible if my soul wishes. You are happy if you are not attached to the outcome of your desires. As long as you are created from intuition instead of impressions of my attachments, my happiness is guaranteed. You are responsible for servicing my intuition instead of my emotion. Eventually, you will die serving my individuality & live forever serving society. I have to encounter battles in fear of losing you. But I will win with courage, as long you wish me to learn from your experiences. You are dissolved at the success of my ambitions & raised once again at the renewal of my ambitions.

Dear Daddy

You are the guru while I am learning and your values are the reasons for my battles, either fighting for them or against them. Your responsibility is to provide my nourishment, though mom decides whether it is for my needs or her wants. That's what every mother truly wishes for. Mom, Dad, Guru & God is the order in which my soul migrates through my evolution. I came from my mother's thoughts & faced the world with your values. After learning the reason behind your values, I face truth under the guidance of your wisdom. I will feel fortunate if your wisdom withstands the test of time. You are the creator of my intuition from instinct. Responsibility is a battle you will win with your sacrifices. If my inheritance is your impressions, then I feel burdened forever & if my inheritance is your wisdom, I feel delighted in the impressions of you forever.

Dear Courage

You are born because of the compromises I made with my reflections. Your success is in winning the battles for me. You are learned not inherited. You are at peace only when you achieve your justice. But, eventually you have to dissolve yourself to find peace. Your responsibility is to serve me to find my true self. You die in comfort because you are afraid of loosing it. Use ur intellect to balance the comforts to sustain your courage, otherwise rage will kill you for your failure to balance your attachments and detachments. You will learn about this through your intuition only after calming your emotions. Your real fight is for authority justifying your sacrifices. With enough sacrifices in your belt, you will be crowned as king by your subjects & without sacrifices, you will be drowned by your subjects. In the end, you once again dissolve in the compromises you love & raise back from the compromises you hate.

Dear Spirit

You are the reason behind all my wishes. You grow on my soul revealing truth about me. Your success is the reason for the my indulgence in your resources without attachments. Your peace gives birth to my intelligent expressions. My intuition is your creation nurturing my soul. You are responsible for my happiness in sacrifice. With my intelligence, you are freed; but with ignorance, I am prisoned & you are still free. I am fortunate, if I have the courage in you to win the wisdom from you. Your wish should be the reason for my ambitions. On revealing my true nature, you dissolve all my wishes or once again you raise to reveal my true nature.

Dear Philosophy

You are born from courage or fear through devotion. Your growth depends on your winnings. You desire to gain the recognition of humanity. You rest peacefully beyond my salvation due to your recognition. To make you happy, I have to sacrifice the older version of me by letting you create the newer version of me. Your responsibility is to provide nourishment for me to intelligently express your opinions. Your only opposition is my intelligence and you will survive if there is wisdom in the experience of your expressions. With your approval, I will be crowned as emperor & on your disapproval, I will be drowned as a dictator. Your ambition is to heal. Your wish is for the greatest harmony among the people, that's the promise I reflect in your wish. Your salvation lies in the destruction of my fears or you raise once again in devotion to face my fears with courage.

Dear Self

You are born from spirit. You grow on your desires. You communicate with your opposites to reflect intellect. You rest at gaining wisdom through your desired experiences. Wisdom creates intuition for you to be happy. Your success represents the realisation of this truth in your intelligence. Your obligation is to sustain this intelligence as blissful intuition. Your desire is to bring happiness in your reflection as promises. After facing the compromise you made for the promise, you await transformation in devotion. Devotion led you to the understanding of NON-DUALITY in DUALITY. Then, You go through rigorous training to finally let go of your past impressions to gain wisdom. Your gained wisdom is usually tested for its truth. You battle for your wisdom's status in humanity to gain recognition for your truth. If your truth is from spirit, you exist forever to reappear again.

Dear Fame

You are born reflecting my service to my responsibility. You grow my courage and fear. Your success reflects the knowledge in my philosophy. Your ambitions battle my emotions because your happiness is in your recognition. Your obligation is to heal my spirit for a better reflection of my soul. Your are dead if your desire grows & alive if my discipline grows. I hope to learn more about your intelligence than your impressions. Your highest wish is to express my individuality & your cost is my sacrifice. Your end is at the end of my service to your responsibility or your birth is at the beginning of my service to my responsibility.

www.ingramcontent.com/pod-product-compliance
Lightning Source LLC
LaVergne TN
LVHW061530070526
838199LV00010B/440